CONVERGE
Bible Studies

FASTING

Bible Studies

FASTING

ASHLEE ALLEY

Abingdon Press

Nashville

FASTING
CONVERGE BIBLE STUDIES

By Ashlee Alley

Library of Congress Cataloging-in-Publication Data has been requested.

ISBN: 978-1-4267-9556-5

Series Editor: Shane Raynor

14 15 16 17 18 19 20 21 22 23—10 9 8 7 6 5 4 3 2 1

Manufactured in the United States of America

CONTENTS

ABOUT THE SERIES

Converge is a series of topical Bible studies based on the Common English Bible translation. Each title in the *Converge* series consists of four studies based around a common topic or theme. *Converge* brings together a unique group of writers from different backgrounds, traditions, and age groups.

HOW TO USE THESE STUDIES

Converge Bible studies can be used by small groups, classes, or individuals. Each study uses a simple format. For the convenience of the reader, the primary Scripture passages are included. In Insight and Ideas, the author of the study explores each Scripture passage, going deeper into the text and helping readers understand how the Scripture connects with the theme of the study. Questions are designed to encourage both personal reflection and group conversation. Some questions may not have simple answers. That's part of what makes studying the Bible so exciting.

Although Bible passages are included with each session, study participants may find it useful to have personal Bibles on hand for referencing other Scriptures. *Converge* studies are designed for use with the Common English Bible; but they work well with any modern, reliable translation.

ONLINE EXTRAS

Converge studies are available in both print and digital formats. Each title in the series has additional components that are available online, including related blog posts and podcasts.

To access the companion materials, visit

http://www.MinistryMatters.com/Converge

Thanks for using *Converge*!

INTRODUCTION

I've served in campus ministry for more than a decade.
I spent most of that time serving as the director of a
discipleship program that had, at its core, instruction in the
spiritual disciplines. One year I was trying to recruit a bright
young man who was the son of a pastor. I ran into his
dad after I'd learned that the student would be attending
another college and felt comfortable asking him about
something that had troubled me since his son's campus visit.
At some point during our conversation when the student
was on campus, I got the impression that he was writing
off the program to which I was inviting him to belong. I'd
remembered being surprised, as he seemed like a great
fit. He was an active part of the ministry in his church, he
had begun to identify a call to ministry, and he seemed to
have many things in common with the students who are
most content in the program that I directed. His dad finally
confessed that his son had been turned off by the use of
the words *spiritual discipline*. Apparently, the student had

never heard the phrase before and had perceived it to imply a holier-than-thou attitude of self-righteousness and of being uptight. Nothing his dad could say could convince him otherwise. This prospective student may not have liked the sound of it, but discipline is spiritual; and it is an important aspect of becoming a disciple of Jesus.

Discipline isn't something that we naturally gravitate toward; but if we are serious about becoming disciples of Jesus, it is something that we must begin to understand. There are a variety of spiritual disciplines with which we have a great deal of familiarity: prayer, Bible study, worship, service. However, I would venture a guess that we would identify the spiritual discipline of fasting among the most confusing, difficult, and undesirable of them. In fact, for many people, fasting is the thing that we do before blood work so as to get the right read on our blood sugar. It's just not something that is a common practice, and we can understand why: Fasting is difficult. Yet making a commitment to lay aside our human desires for a time of being filled with the work of prayer, self-reflection, and sacrifice makes us more faithful followers of Jesus.

One reason we tend to have such a difficult time with fasting today is that we have such complicated issues with food. Food is nearly ubiquitous in America, yet 17.2 million households (or 14.5 percent of households) are considered food insecure. Still, nearly 70 percent of Americans are overweight. This contrast may be emblematic of our spiritual lives. We often neglect certain spiritual practices which are confusing, difficult, and require a sacrifice but then partake in those that fill us up and make us feel good, loved, and accepted. I am not saying that we should not feel good, loved, and accepted. However, we cannot truly know the fullness of what it means to be a Christian unless we understand firsthand the concept of what it means to be empty of ourselves so that we can be filled with Christ.

John Wesley's well known "Covenant Prayer" includes the line "Let me be full; let me be empty. Let me have all things; let me have nothing. I freely and heartily yield all things to your pleasure and disposal." Perhaps he cultivated the ability to pray this through his regular practice of fasting. Wesley was known to fast twice weekly; and in the early years of his ministry, he joined with his fellow members of the group that was dubbed the "Holy Club" for their fasting. Their spiritual practices undergirded their personal faith and their visible ministry and led to a renewal of faith that spread all over the world in a relatively few short years.

The texts for this study will help you identify several different aspects of fasting. You will examine a rationale for fasting, learn about how fasting was practiced in the context of biblical history, and discover some practical aspects of fasting when you're ready to undertake the fast yourself. Some practical ideas are sprinkled throughout; but in the last lesson, you can get a glimpse of steps that you can undertake to begin learning about and practicing fasting. I've also included some of John Wesley's thoughts on fasting throughout the study in addition to the Scripture lessons.

My experience with fasting has paralleled my experiences with regular exercise for most of my adult life. Throughout this study, I'll reference lessons that I've learned through regular exercise, specifically running, that have given me insight into the spiritual discipline of fasting. The key is the commitment to the discipline. Likewise, fasting requires discipline. It involves the body, but it is mostly about the head and the heart.

However, another parallel between running and fasting is that it isn't for everyone. My friends with bad knees or hips should find another exercise that is easier on the mechanics of their body. Likewise, I have friends who should not engage in fasting. People who have struggled with an eating disorder or who are diabetic may need to find another spiritual practice that allows them to connect with God but doesn't put their body or mind in the vulnerable position that is inherent in fasting.

The point of fasting is not about a legalistic restriction of food. Rather, it is about finding ways to submit even one's most basic human desires to God in order to experience the fulfillment of a life with Christ that takes us beyond our circumstances. Throughout this study, I pray that you would be encouraged to contemplate more deeply the way of a life focused on God. May God meet you in the quiet places that are possible in the desert places of a fast. And may you find an abundance that fills you unto satisfaction!

1

AVOIDING SHOWY RELIGION
A HEART FOCUSED ON THE THINGS OF GOD

SCRIPTURE
MATTHEW 6:1-18

[1]"Be careful that you don't practice your religion in front of people to draw their attention. If you do, you will have no reward from your Father who is in heaven.

[2]"Whenever you give to the poor, don't blow your trumpet as the hypocrites do in the synagogues and in the streets so that they may get praise from people. I assure you, that's the only reward they'll get. [3]But when you give to the poor, don't let your left hand know what your right hand is doing [4]so that you may give to the poor in secret. Your Father who sees what you do in secret will reward you.

[5]"When you pray, don't be like hypocrites. They love to pray standing in the synagogues and on the street corners so that people will see them. I assure you, that's the only reward they'll get. [6]But when you pray, go to your room, shut the door, and pray to your Father who is present in that secret place. Your Father who sees what you do in secret will reward you.

[7]"When you pray, don't pour out a flood of empty words, as the Gentiles do. They think that by saying many words they'll be heard. [8]Don't be like them, because your Father knows what you need before you ask. [9]Pray like this:

Our Father who is in heaven,
uphold the holiness of your name.
[10]Bring in your kingdom
so that your will is done on earth as it's done in heaven.
[11]Give us the bread we need for today.
[12]Forgive us for the ways we have wronged you,
just as we also forgive those who have wronged us.
[13]And don't lead us into temptation,
but rescue us from the evil one.

[14]"If you forgive others their sins, your heavenly Father will also forgive you. [15]But if you don't forgive others, neither will your Father forgive your sins.

[16]"And when you fast, don't put on a sad face like the hypocrites. They distort their faces so people will know they are fasting. I

assure you that they have their reward. [17]When you fast, brush your hair and wash your face. [18]Then you won't look like you are fasting to people, but only to your Father who is present in that secret place. Your Father who sees in secret will reward you.

INSIGHT AND IDEAS

I saw a meme come across Facebook the other day that made me laugh and cringe at the same time. "Thank goodness for Facebook! Otherwise, I'd have to call all of my friends in order to tell them that I went running today!" You see, I've been a runner off and on (mostly off) for more than a decade until the last two years. Now I've been fairly committed to running three to four times a week. So I know both sides of the story. When you've had a really great, long run (which may sound like an impossibility to some people), you want to share your experience with others. And yes, there's something about knowing that you just ran (3, 4, 5, 13) miles that is so empowering. You may call it bragging; I call it the effect of endorphins.

And yet it does get annoying to read updates from people who don't quite make my Christmas card list, telling me how many miles they just ran and how it "hurts so good." It can start to feel like they're bragging, shaming others, and looking for pats on the back. And "we" just don't like it. I've learned from being a fairly committed runner that some things are better left unsaid.

SHOWING OFF

Jesus pointed this out to us, too, though not about running. He understood the tendency we have to announce our accomplishments when it comes to our religious behavior and gave some instruction in Matthew 6 about showy religion. Jesus used three different examples, and each one makes the same point: Don't practice your faith as a way to show off, impress people, or impress God. Jesus talked about giving financially to the poor, praying, and fasting. These are three important behaviors that draw us closer to God but aren't effective in that goal when they are merely rote actions.

Let's take helping the poor, for example. Giving financially gives me an opportunity to support God's work in the world around me. I can even be an answer to someone else's prayer when I notice a need or simply feel compelled to give someone some money. When I tithe, I'm challenged to prioritize my spending so that the work of my local church—and even the church around the world through my church's giving—can continue. Giving regularly increases my dependence on God, sometimes for my financial needs to be met and sometimes to find my satisfaction in God rather in the "stuff" that I would buy if I didn't give to God. All of these are really important by-products of giving. But what if I were to give to the poor and then announce it on Facebook? According to this teaching by Jesus in Matthew 6, I would be getting my reward through "likes" and not from God.

If God doesn't want us to let others know about our giving, does that mean that we need to remove all of those little plaques from our pianos, pulpits, and pews in our churches? Well, maybe. I'll leave that for you to decide; but it does mean that we need to consider what motivates us to do the things we do, especially as it relates to sacrificial living in the Christian life. Jesus' specific advice is this: "But when you give to the poor, don't let your left hand know what your right hand is doing so that you may give to the poor in secret. Your Father who sees what you do in secret will reward you" (Matthew 6:3-4).

PAYING ATTENTION

I'm not the most coordinated person in the world, but the only way that I can imagine not letting my left hand know what my right hand is doing is for my action of giving to the poor to become so natural that I don't even have to think about it. I just do it. The same thing goes for praying and, maybe more difficultly, for fasting. Is it possible that our spiritual behaviors can become something that is so natural that it's almost reflexive?

I said earlier that these are three important behaviors that draw us closer to God, but they aren't effective in that goal when they are merely rote actions. It's a natural temptation to turn something into a mindless, rote activity. Running, driving, and even flying planes. OK, for most of us, flying planes isn't a rote, mindless activity; but the concept of going on autopilot is something that we say all the time. In flying airplanes, there are computers that monitor the important information such as airspeed, altitude, equipment, and weather. These computers actually increase the safety of the flight over a human pilot because they indicate when changes need to be made or they just make the changes automatically. When we hear the rare stories of pilots of commercial jets who have fallen asleep or who are playing games on their phones, we're grateful for autopilot even if we're outraged at the lack of paying attention. You see, paying attention is what Jesus wants us to do in these spiritual practices. We may not be taking others' lives into our hands (the way a pilot does) when we give to the poor, pray, or fast; but the intentionality of how we engage these practices is what allows us to connect with God, and that's where we'll get our reward.

Rather than allowing ourselves to go on autopilot, however, can we truly get to a point where our spiritual behaviors are reflexive? If so, then continued practice of these spiritual disciplines will reshape our hearts and minds so that we can guard against practicing a rote activity and exhibit a natural activity, where our engagement simply happens again because we've engaged with it so many times in the past.

WHEN YOU FAST...

Jesus says another thing in this passage that is worth drawing attention to. When he's teaching, he doesn't sound like it's even an option whether to give to the poor, pray, or fast. In fact, in Matthew 6:16, he said "*When* you fast," not *if* you fast. Oops!

As we turn our attention to the importance of fasting, I'm not about to heap extra guilt or false expectations on us. But here's what I hope to do. I hope to crack open the ancient practice/mystery of fasting that can shape us as Christians into people who more closely resemble Christ. All that *because of restricting food*, you say? *Surely, you overpromise!*

TIMES FOR FASTING

Well, I'll let you be the judge; but for now, consider how the very first listeners, Jesus' Jewish audience, would have heard this instruction about fasting. They knew all about fasting. As a community, they all celebrated one very special day each year when the entire community was fasting, the Day of Atonement (Leviticus 23:26-29). This was the day that, even if you weren't an especially devout follower, you still observed a fast and worshipped. It's not likely that Jesus was speaking to the Jews about this day, because there would have been no need to announce that you were fasting, because *everyone* was fasting. Rather, Jesus was likely speaking to the number of faithful Jews who observed the other minor holy days or even practiced fasting as a way of showing their own righteousness. Perhaps Jesus was speaking to the tendency that we have to compare, compete, and try to prove ourselves to God and others.

There were other reasons Jews would have fasted at times other than the appointed fast days. They would have fasted for repentance (Deuteronomy 9:15-18; Jonah 3:4-10; 1 Kings 21:17-29), in making war (Judges 20:26), when interceding for someone (2 Samuel 12:16-23), and in preparation for something significant (Esther 4:16). With the exception of making war, these are all practices that bring a person in deeper faithfulness as he or she walks with God but would also be greatly respected and admired. Were the people of Jesus' days patting themselves on their backs just a little too hard?

PARTIAL FASTS

When we think of fasting, we tend to think of giving up all food during a set-aside time. Certainly this "complete fast" is specified in various references to fasting in Scripture; but at other times, the fast is a partial fast.

Daniel and his friends' eating the diet of vegetables and water rather than enjoying the wine and extravagant diet of the king's table is an example of a partial fast (Daniel 1). This kind of fast may be something you've experienced if you've given something up for Lent. A partial fast gives a taste of what you might experience on a complete fast; and it also serves an important purpose in teaching discipline, especially as it relates to one particular area.

REASONS FOR FASTING

While the actions of fasting—overruling our physical desires to connect more deeply with God—are important, what Jesus is speaking to is the state of our hearts. It seems that some in Jesus' audience had missed the point of the fasting. Fasting is not about drawing attention to yourself and looking more religious; it's about becoming naturally in tune with God so that the "left hand [doesn't] know what [the] right hand is doing."

My own motivation for fasting in my Christian life has been varied: seeking wisdom, obedience, a deeper intimacy with God, and even repentance. But while all of these are good reasons for fasting, they can't be primary. All other motivation must be subject to this one: to glorify God. John Wesley, the founder of Methodism, incorporated fasting in his life on a regular basis. He believed that it was an essential practice of faith development in the lives of those who want to grow deeper in their faith. He underscored the primary motivation of fasting like this:

> Let our intention herein be this, and this alone, to glorify our Father which is in heaven; to express our sorrow and shame for our manifold transgressions of his holy law; to wait for an increase of purifying grace, drawing our affections to things above; to add seriousness and earnestness to our prayers; to avert the wrath of God, and to obtain all the great and precious promises which he hath made to us in Jesus Christ.[1]

Fasting is an avenue for living a life of holiness. It's not the act of denying one's food that does the sanctifying. Rather, there is something powerful about denying a part of one's desires that makes us able to take up the desires of God.

From running long distances I have learned that when I am training regularly, I am better able to do difficult, solo work. Running and doing hard work don't seem related. However,

---

1. "Upon Our Lord's Sermon on the Mount: Discourse Seven," Sermon 27 from *The Sermons of John Wesley*; http://wesley.nnu.edu/john-wesley/the-sermons-of-john-wesley-1872-edition/sermon-27-upon-our-lords-sermon-on-the-mount-discourse-seven. Accessed 2 July 2014.

training myself to stay focused and keep moving one foot after another one has cultivated in me the ability to stay engaged in the project I'm working on, work a bit longer, send a few more e-mails. Don't get me wrong. It hasn't trained me to become a workaholic; it has trained me to stay focused in a way that it actually takes less time to do the work that is most important.

By submitting to a regular, challenging, spiritually-focused activity, we're able to be shaped by God, to be transformed into the people that God is calling us to be (Romans 12:1-2). While discipline may feel restrictive, it really is about a sense of freedom on the other side of that discipline. The freedom I've experienced is that after the discipline of running four days a week, I can go run a fun 5K with friends without training. Likewise, there's a spiritual parallel. By practicing a spiritual discipline, one develops the endurance to meet the challenges of life more attuned to God's voice, respond with God's character, and see the challenges from God's perspective.

The practice of fasting is a way to glorify God. But just like announcing our exercises on Facebook turns people off, so does announcing our spiritual accomplishments. And when the primary goal of fasting is to glorify God, we may have reached our goal yet completely missed the point.

QUESTIONS

1. What does Matthew 6:1 say about practicing one's religion in front of people? When is this a bad thing?

2. What is the reward Jesus mentions in Matthew 6:1?

3. How do you do something without letting the left hand know what the right hand is doing (Matthew 6:3)?

4. How does one balance giving in secret with instructing other believers on giving by our example (Matthew 6:4)?

5. What implications does Matthew 6:5-6 have for public prayer? How do we pray publicly without praying like the hypocrites that Jesus mentions? Are private prayers more effective than public ones? Why, or why not?

6. What role does language pray in prayer? How important are the words we say? What might Jesus be saying about how long believers should pray (Matthew 6:7-8)?

7. What role should the Lord's Prayer play in the prayer life of a Christian (Matthew 6:9-13)?

8. What does the Lord's Prayer tell us about God's kingdom and God's will? How do these connect with our prayers?

9. How is forgiving others tied to receiving forgiveness from God (Matthew 6:12, 14)?

10. Is it possible for God to lead us into temptation (Matthew 6:13)? What might this verse reveal about prayer and its effect on malevolent spiritual forces?

11. When would it be appropriate to tell others that you're fasting? When would it be inappropriate (Matthew 6:6-18)?

2

FASTING AND PRAYING
PREPARATION FOR THE WORK AHEAD

SCRIPTURE
ACTS 13:1-5; 14:21-28

ACTS 13:1-5

¹The church at Antioch included prophets and teachers: Barnabas, Simeon (nicknamed Niger), Lucius from Cyrene, Manaen (a childhood friend of Herod the ruler), and Saul. ²As they were worshipping the Lord and fasting, the Holy Spirit said, "Appoint Barnabas and Saul to the work I have called them to undertake." ³After they fasted and prayed, they laid their hands on these two and sent them off.

⁴After the Holy Spirit sent them on their way, they went down to Seleucia. From there they sailed to Cyprus. ⁵In Salamis they proclaimed God's word in the Jewish synagogues. John was with them as their assistant.

ACTS 14:21-28

²¹Paul and Barnabas proclaimed the good news to the people in Derbe and made many disciples. Then they returned to Lystra, Iconium, and Antioch, where ²²they strengthened the disciples and urged them to remain firm in the faith. They told them, "If we are to enter God's kingdom, we must pass through many troubles." ²³They appointed elders for each church. With prayer and fasting, they committed these elders to the Lord, in whom they had placed their trust.

²⁴After Paul and Barnabas traveled through Pisidia, they came to Pamphylia. ²⁵They proclaimed the word in Perga, then went down to Attalia. ²⁶From there they sailed to Antioch, where they had been entrusted by God's grace to the work they had now completed. ²⁷On their arrival, they gathered the church together and reported everything that God had accomplished through their activity, and how God had opened a door of faith for the Gentiles. ²⁸They stayed with the disciples a long time.

INSIGHT AND IDEAS

Most of us have some sort of ritual to fuel us in the midst of things that require a particular level of focus. Ask a musician, and he'll tell you that he visualizes his performance. Ask an athlete, and she'll tell you about her mental checklist and her lucky socks. Ask a preacher, and he'll tell you about the song he jams to on his way to the church. Often, how we prepare for something is the crucial piece in our ability to defeat the psychological components of any difficult task. Sure, there are elements of physical preparation; but what happens when the biggest battle is the internal one?

At one point during training for a half-marathon, I discovered an unexpected battle over food: If I ate too close to the beginning of my workout, I felt sick; but if I ate too early, I didn't have the power to finish the long run. There are lots of products that I could buy that would fuel me with "quick energy"; but unfortunately, I couldn't stand how they tasted. So I found myself in a bit of a quandary about how to prepare to have enough steam to finish a long run.

One Saturday before I ran, I finally stumbled upon the perfect balance: Half a bagel with peanut butter and half of a banana one hour before I ran. The payoff of my experiment was that I felt great during my whole run. Now, there are probably a number of food items that I could eat an hour prior to a workout, with a similar balance of carbs and protein; but this is what worked for me once, and so now it has become my ritual. So I dare not stray from it.

I think that we do pregame rituals, make checklists, and go through a routine because somehow it allows us to feel like we can control something. Often, we don't feel that we can control the outcome of the game, the feelings of anxiety about a big performance, or how well a sermon is received; so we do what we can to prepare well.

PREPARING OURSELVES

Fasting is a part of how we can spiritually prepare ourselves to be attentive to God's work in our lives. I remember a time when I was in the midst of quite a bit of turmoil related to what I sensed God calling me to do. I was working for a ministry, but things were very difficult; and I was struggling to know whether God was calling me to attend seminary. I knew that, perhaps, I simply wanted to leave the difficulty of my current situation; yet I felt a sense of calling to attend seminary. I had previously been exposed to the concept of fasting. The little that I knew at the time was that fasting was a way to seek God's will and to purify and get to the bottom of one's desires. I felt a sense of leading by God to enter into a time of fasting as I was seeking God's will and preparing to make an important decision.

New Year's Day was approaching, so I decided to begin the new year by fasting and praying until I had heard from God about the decision that was at hand. I remember waking each day with a sense of expecting to hear from God, of deep commitment to seeking God, of allowing my pangs of hunger or physical weakness to be a reminder of my dependence upon God. I spent two days reading Scripture, praying, and singing songs—probably badly, but it didn't matter as I was simply making "a joyful noise unto the Lord" (Psalm 98:4; 100:1, NRSV). I wrote in my journal and read a book about deeper discipleship. And I fasted. And it wasn't easy. I remember that I went back to work on the third day of my fast; and as I did, I got the clarity that I was seeking and had a sense of God's leading me to apply to seminary for the coming fall semester. I broke my fast that evening with a simple dinner and began to have a deeper sense of God's direction in my life from that time on.

The fasting experience prepared my heart to make a decision. I still had to enact that decision—determine which seminary I would attend, wrap up the ministry that I had led for two years, and pack up to move halfway across the country—but my heart was sure, even when I struggled with the many objections to the challenges that were involved.

FASTING IN THE EARLY CHURCH

You see, fasting prepares our hearts and our minds for challenging actions. We see in Scripture where the preparation for beginning a new chapter in life included fasting. In Acts, we read of many times when the early Christian church practiced fasting. Paul's story gives us some great illustrations. Paul, who was called Saul, had a rather dramatic conversion, which is recounted in Acts 9. Prior to that, he was an ardent Jew, persecuting the Christians, who were a threat to the Jewish status quo. At the time of his conversion, this enemy of the faith was pulled into the community of the Christian church for what we could imagine as a time of growth, discipleship, and sharing with the other Christians in understanding of the revolutionary work that Jesus had done. In fact, Acts 9:31 says, "Then the church throughout Judea, Galilee, and Samaria enjoyed a time of peace. God strengthened the church, and its life was marked by reverence for the Lord. Encouraged by the Holy Spirit, the church continued to grow in numbers."

We pick back up on Saul's story in chapter 13, where it seems that the Christian community is doing what they do—worshipping and fasting—and the Holy Spirit interrupts them to give them a message: "Appoint Barnabas and Saul to the work that I have called them to undertake." These are the first steps of Paul's recorded ministry, and the author of Acts hasn't even started calling him Paul yet (his name is indicated as Paul a few verses later, in verse 9). It seems to indicate that fasting and worship are common experiences of these early Christians; and when they fast, they hear from the Holy Spirit in specific detail.

HEARING GOD'S VOICE

Fasting has a way of amplifying God's voice. Perhaps it's the way that a person learns to listen more deeply through denying the physical pangs of hunger. Perhaps it's because through fasting, one perseveres despite feeling a sense of weakness. Perhaps it's the weakness itself that reorients what is most important and allows us to dismiss the easy answers in search for the right ones. We know from this passage in Acts that it was through fasting and praying that the believers in Antioch heard God's voice for Paul and Barnabas to enter into ministry. And guess what they did next. They fasted and prayed again.

Although the text doesn't say anything about the amount of time that passed between when they got the word from the Holy Spirit and when they launched Paul and Barnabas into ministry, I think it's safe to assume that they underwent another time of preparation that included fasting and prayer prior to launching out into ministry to the Gentiles.

In my own experience prior to making a life changing decision, fasting is what allowed me to cultivate the ability to turn down the other voices vying for my attention and to focus on only God's voice. However, I don't think that fasting is reserved for only the big decisions of life, but for cultivating a life of attentiveness to God. Out of Paul's missionary journey came an opportunity—not only for Paul, but for others who replicated that missionary journey.

We hear the end of this particular missionary journey in Acts 14:21-28. We see a pattern as they ended their journey in the same way that they started it: with fasting and prayer. "They appointed elders for each church. With prayer and fasting, they committed these elders to the Lord, in whom they had placed their trust" (Acts 14:23). There was a vitality in the life of these early Christians. It was a vibrancy and dynamism that was a result of their sacrifice, their practices, and their shared vision. You see, fasting doesn't just prepare us for something; it prepares us to live each day launched into the ministry to which God calls us. Fasting, then, need not be a practice only for special occasions. It can be a sustainable practice that finds its way into our lives on a regular basis.

CONNECTING WITH GOD

Fasting isn't a sacrificial deed to earn God's favor. It is a joyful act to connect with God. The Book of Acts itself is a narrative of the life of the earliest Christians after the ascension of Christ. It marks how they shaped community; the lives of the church leaders; and particularly relevant

31

for this passage, the missionary journeys of Paul. Each time fasting is mentioned in the Book of Acts, it is paired with prayer. As a budding Christian community, fasting was simply a common part of their expression of faith. And what a vibrant faith it was! Prayer and fasting were instrumental in helping these Christian leaders stand up to the challenges for which Jesus had prepared them. Leaders were committed to the Lord with prayer and fasting (Acts 14:23). And more than that, they were exhibiting a life marked by joy.

In Acts 13:52, in the midst of this missionary journey, this note is made referencing Paul and Barnabas on their journey: "Because of the abundant presence of the Holy Spirit in their lives, the disciples were overflowing with happiness." That is saying something impressive, considering the stories of harassment, sacrifice, and uncertainty that they were experiencing.

Fasting isn't about earning God's favor. Yet it is definitely an avenue of God's blessing. John Wesley kept this in perspective in his writing on fasting:

> We cannot be too often warned of this; inasmuch as a desire to "establish our own righteousness," to procure salvation of debt and not of grace, is so deeply rooted in all our hearts. Fasting is only a way which God hath ordained, wherein we wait for his unmerited mercy; and wherein, without any desert of ours, he hath promised freely to give us his blessing.[1]

---

1. From Sermon 27, in *The Works of the Rev. John Wesley, A.M.,* Volume 1, by John Wesley, edited by John Emory (B. Waugh and T. Mason, 1835); page 254.

I work with college students; and a significant part of what happens in the college years is about preparation: preparing for a career; preparing for graduate school; and in some cases, preparing for marriage. I often tell students that they're not just preparing for life after college; they're actually living life now. While this is true, the choices that they make now are what open up the doors that are available to them after they have prepared. If they've prepared well for their careers, they'll be more likely to find a job that connects their passions with the needs in the world. If they've prepared well in their studies, they can pursue graduate school. If they've prepared well in their relationships, they will be able to navigate challenges that will inevitably come their way. Likewise, the preparation that we do is both an encounter with God as we do it and an opportunity to be equipped for future steps of faith.

Fasting prepares our hearts and minds for challenging action. It has a way of amplifying God's voice. And it is not a sacrificial deed to earn God's favor, but a joyful act to connect with God. May it not just prepare you for something, but may it prepare all of us to live each day launched by the Holy Spirit into the ministry to which God calls us each and every day!

QUESTIONS

1. In what ways is the Holy's Spirit's speaking in Acts 13:2 connected with the worship and fasting that preceded it?

2. How does the Holy Spirit speak today? What can we do to hear the Holy Spirit's voice more clearly?

3. What role should fasting and prayer play today in selecting Christian leaders and supporting their ministries?

4. How did Paul and Barnabas strengthen the disciples in Lystra, Iconium, and Antioch (Acts 14:22)? Why did they say that to enter God's kingdom, we must pass through many troubles?

5. Who are the elders that are appointed in Acts 14:23? Who are the elders in the church today?

6. Why, do you think, does fasting help us be more attentive to God?

7. What is the difference between a routine fast and a special fast? What are the spiritual benefits of each? How do we know when a special fast might be necessary?

8. How does fasting make us weaker? How does it make us stronger? Why are both of these important?

9. Why does fasting seem to amplify God's voice? What have been your experiences with fasting in this regard?

10. Should Christians see fasting as a way to get God's attention? Why, or why not?

3

FASTING FROM INJUSTICE
OPENING THE DOOR TO GOD'S BLESSINGS

SCRIPTURE
ISAIAH 58:1-14

[1]Shout loudly; don't hold back;
  raise your voice like a trumpet!
Announce to my people their crime,
  to the house of Jacob their sins.
[2]They seek me day after day,
  desiring knowledge of my ways
  like a nation that acted righteously,
  that didn't abandon their God.
They ask me for righteous judgments,
  wanting to be close to God.
[3]"Why do we fast and you don't see;
  why afflict ourselves and you don't notice?"

Yet on your fast day

you do whatever you want,

and oppress all your workers.

4You quarrel and brawl, and then you fast;

you hit each other violently with your fists.

You shouldn't fast as you are doing today

if you want to make your voice heard on high.

5Is this the kind of fast I choose,

a day of self-affliction,

of bending one's head like a reed

and of lying down in mourning clothing and ashes?

Is this what you call a fast, a day acceptable to the Lord?

6Isn't this the fast I choose:

releasing wicked restraints, untying the ropes of a yoke,

setting free the mistreated,

and breaking every yoke?

7Isn't it sharing your bread with the hungry

and bringing the homeless poor into your house,

covering the naked when you see them,

and not hiding from your own family?

8Then your light

will break out like the dawn,

and you will be healed quickly.

Your own righteousness

will walk before you,

and the Lord's glory will be your rear guard.

⁹Then you will call,

and the LORD will answer;

you will cry for help, and God will say, "I'm here."

If you remove the yoke from among you,

the finger-pointing, the wicked speech;

¹⁰if you open your heart to the hungry,

and provide abundantly for those who are afflicted,

your light will shine in the darkness,

and your gloom will be like the noon.

¹¹The LORD will guide you continually

and provide for you, even in parched places.

He will rescue your bones.

You will be like a watered garden,

like a spring of water that won't run dry.

¹²They will rebuild ancient ruins

on your account;

the foundations of generations past you will restore.

You will be called

Mender of Broken Walls,

Restorer of Livable Streets.

¹³If you stop trampling the Sabbath,

stop doing whatever you want on my holy day,

and consider the Sabbath a delight,

sacred to the LORD, honored,

and honor it instead of doing things your way,

seeking what you want and doing business as usual,

[14]then you will take delight

   in the LORD.

I will let you ride on the heights

   of the earth;

I will sustain you with the heritage

   of your ancestor Jacob.

INSIGHT AND IDEAS

I totally get that runners can be obnoxious. I've actually heard runners say, "I can't wait to post this workout on Facebook!" Yeah, that annoys me, too. But I understand why runners want to brag about it. Running is hard work. It is for the elite: Not just anyone can run long distances—or so we think.

Now, before you skewer me, keep reading. Running is also about health, setting and reaching a challenging goal, and finding inner strength. Since I started running on a regular basis, I have begun to identify it as a spiritual discipline. That may sound strange. Let me explain.

Robert Mulholland, emeritus professor of New Testament at Asbury Theological Seminary, says that spiritual formation is the "process of being conformed to the image of Christ for the sake of others."[1] It may seem that running is something that benefits only the runner (and perhaps an organization

---

1. From *Invitation to a Journey: A Road Map for Spiritual Formation,* by M. Robert Mulholland, Jr., (InterVarsity Press, 1993); Page 15.

holding a fund-raising race to raise some moolah from all of the crazy runners). However, the effects of running carry over into a runner's life in other ways. Perhaps she is able to push through difficult circumstances because she has cultivated an inner strength from pushing her body past what she thought was her limit. Perhaps his physical health is stronger because he stays in a healthy weight range due to regular exercise. Perhaps her psychological world is healthier because she has nurtured a habit of weekly exercise even when she didn't want to step out the door. After logging nearly 1,000 miles in the last two years, I have actually learned the secret about running: Running is hard work. But it's not really just for the elite. With time and commitment, anyone can learn to run long distances. In fact, by joining with others, it may even inspire someone else to take the steps (literally) to reach new horizons (figuratively). And I'm not just talking about the ones over the highway. The truths that one can discover through sustained physical exercise have significant spiritual parallels.

The practice of fasting is one that could easily fall into the same category as running as far as its difficulty/impressiveness factor. Anyone who has ever tried a diet recognizes how difficult it is to restrict food and the weakness that one feels when breaking a food-related addiction. Fasting is hard work. It is for the elite: Not just anyone can go without food for long periods of time. In fact, by telling others about it, it may even inspire others to fast (literally) to reach new horizons (figuratively).

41

A LENTEN LESSON

One of my first encounters with fasting came to be because of a Lenten season. My limited exposure to Lent while I was growing up was from my friends who were Catholic. Most memorably, I had one friend who gave up chocolate each year because she didn't like it; but it sounded really impressive that she gave up something that most people love. Thus my impressions of Lent were fairly low—until college. During college, I was taught that Lent is a season of preparation, where we come face-to-face with our own broken humanity. It starts with the admonition, "From dust you come and to dust you will return." Well, when you put it that way....

I have come to understand Lent as a season (40 days plus Sundays) to prepare my heart and mind to joyfully receive the miracle, the celebration, the proclamation of the resurrection of Christ. The "giving up something for Lent" part reminds me that I have freedom in Christ and stewardship of my body, and that it is all subject to the frailty of humanity. Looking back, I see the many discipleship lessons I've learned during the season of Lent. At times, I've given up a food item. At other times, my sacrifice was something technology- or media-related. I've even *added* a spiritual practice of reading from a particular Gospel daily.

One harrowing Lenten season, I gave up spending money, except on basic needs—housing, gasoline, groceries, and so forth. That meant no eating out during that season and no new Easter outfit, and I even made a baby gift from items I already had because I had committed to not spend money. Learning to lay down certain freedoms during a particular season has been a formative part of my own discipleship throughout the years. However, I can remember one of the first years that I practiced a form of fasting during Lent. I had given up soft drinks, mostly because I thought that I probably had a slight addiction. Each time I bypassed the pop machine and went to the lemonade machine in the college cafeteria, I was pretty proud of my commitment to my "discipline." Then one day, one of my friends who knew that I was giving up pop for Lent said, "Ashlee, aren't you just basically substituting lemonade for pop? It's still a sweet drink." Now, I don't want to get hung up in the spirit of legalism here, but my friend's observation pointed out to me that I was sort of doing a half-hearted attempt at sacrifice during the season of Lent. I was fasting from pop, but was still enjoying a comparable drink. It made my sacrifice seem as arbitrary as not eating orange foods. Sure, it was somewhat of a sacrifice; but instead of eating sweet potato fries, I could just eat regular French fries. Where in that is the reminder that I'm dust?

SEEING 'RESULTS'

This is an oversimplified illustration of the heart of what we see in Isaiah 58. God's people were going through the motions of the fast in an attempt to hear from God, all the while complaining because they weren't seeing results. In my case, I had developed a sense of pride over my spiritual accomplishment. I was expecting to experience God's blessing due to my commitment during Lent. But I had totally missed the point.

The desire to want to "achieve" things that can be reached only through hard work is evident in Isaiah 58. The prophet is instructed to "shout out, do not hold back!" as he announces to God's people their sins (verse 1). Their sin is that they are using fasting as a means to try to manipulate God. Verses 2-3 identify that they have sought God but have not acknowledged their past sins. And it seems that they've even begun to complain to God for God's inattentiveness to their "righteous" behavior. "Why do we fast, but you do not see? Why humble ourselves, but you do not notice?" (Isaiah 58:3a) If they had lived today, they might be inclined to post a Facebook status about this:

> Spent the whole day fasting and *still* haven't heard from God.

Or

> Those extra sackcloth and ashes sure are going to come in handy in the fast I'm getting ready to start. I'll see you on the other side! #fasting #offthegrid

Yeah. We need a prophet to "shout out" to us every now and then. Enter Isaiah. His words can speak to us, too. He chides the people on their lack of integrity in their fast. They meet the standards of the fast; but they do so and oppress their workers, quarrel and brawl, and all together look pitiful (verses 3-5). And their fasting isn't convincing anyone.

Part of the conviction around this passage is that it highlights the criticism that people have about Christians. There seems to be a hypocrisy in their actions. Author and priest Brennan Manning famously said, "The greatest single cause of atheism in the world is Christians who acknowledge Jesus with their lips and walk out the door and deny him with their lifestyle. That is what an unbelieving world simply finds unbelievable."[2] The fasting that the prophet in Isaiah is denouncing is one that is worthy of Manning's criticism. Their religious behavior didn't match up with their actions. This is the fast God doesn't want. It's not hard to understand why.

WHAT DOES GOD WANT?

So what is in the fast that God *does* want?

It seems that in fasting, God wants justice to prevail, the hungry to be filled, family relationships to be reenforced, even healing to take place (Isaiah 58:6-12). This is much better than a bunch of Facebook likes.

It seems that it's human nature to substitute something that looks convincing for that which really is true. We convince ourselves that a shortcut or close second is good enough. The vision that Isaiah casts about fasting is one where there is no substitute for the real thing. The fasting that God chooses unites fasting with liberation, justice for the poor, hospitality, feeding and clothing the poor, and personal

---

2. See *http://www.brainyquote.com/quotes/quotes/b/brennanman531776.html*. Accessed 2 July 2014.

healing. It is a spiritual act that restores relationship with God, brings righteousness, and sets a person free from the things that typically bind us.

This is a weighty promise that God gives through the prophet Isaiah. And yet, what is revealed through fasting really does lead to all of these things. Fasting reveals a significant truth about our humanity. We are hungry, and hungry people become desperate. Oftentimes, the hunger that we feel isn't physical, but rather, it's spiritual. We seek to be accepted by God, by others, even by ourselves. We seek to be loved and to find meaning. We often look to all sorts of other things for this acceptance, love, and meaningfulness. We seek it in financial gain, popularity, success—even at the cost of others. But there is something about fasting that helps us reorient our priorities in this regard. Feeling physical hunger reminds us of who we are in our most basic form and gives us an awareness of how we might learn to depend on God's provision in all of these areas.

The promise the prophet gives about fasting is found in verse 11:

> The Lord will guide you continually
>> and provide for you, even in parched places.
> He will rescue your bones.
> You will be like a watered garden,
>> like a spring of water that won't run dry.

This is a significant vision that the prophet is casting. By practicing scarcity, we can experience abundance. By knowing the depths of despair and need, we will find rescue. By planting seeds of sacrifice, we will reap a harvest of joy. Verse 12 even gives us a new name in the process:

> They will rebuild ancient ruins
>> on your account;
>> the foundations of generations past you will restore.
> You will be called
>> Mender of Broken Walls,
>> Restorer of Livable Streets.

All because of fasting. Yeah, that's way better than Facebook likes.

I've heard people compare fasting to a hunger strike, especially using this dynamic of the relationship of justice to fasting. However, the fast that God chooses is vastly different from a hunger strike. Hunger strikes have been used, even very successfully, to draw attention to important social issues. But a hunger strike is meant to send a very public message that an issue is worth going without even the most basic human need in order to make a difference. A fast, on the other hand, is a very private experience where the message is an individual one. The fast seeks to restore justice through spiritual rather than social means. It isn't about coercion, especially not of God; it's about yielding.

In John Wesley's writing on fasting, he identifies this:

> [Fasting] is chiefly, as it is a help to prayer, that it has so frequently been found a means, in the hand of God, of confirming and increasing, not one virtue, not chastity only, (as some have idly

imagined, without any ground either from Scripture, reason, or experience,) but also seriousness of spirit, earnestness, sensibility and tenderness of conscience, deadness to the world, and consequently the love of God, and every holy and heavenly affection.

Not that there is any natural or necessary connection between fasting, and the blessings God conveys thereby. But he will have mercy *as* he will have mercy; he will convey whatsoever seemeth him good by whatsoever means he is pleased to appoint.[3]

We do experience God's blessings through fasting. We receive anew the joy of the Resurrection on Easter after a long and dark Lenten season. We experience gratitude in the hands that have prepared our food and even in the plants and animals that made it possible. We are blessed as we are reconciled to others and know that injustices are eliminated when we live out the fast of God's choosing.

Fasting is hard work. However, it is not really just for the elite: Anyone can go without food for long periods of time. However, it starts by taking baby steps (figuratively) in order to reach new levels of dependence on the Holy Spirit (literally). Through our fasting, may we see God's provision, even in the parched places. May our lives be springs of water that won't run dry. May we be called Menders of Broken Walls and Restorers of Livable Streets.

Who cares about Facebook likes?

---

3. From Sermon 27, in *The Works of the Rev. John Wesley, A.M.*, Volume 1, by John Wesley, edited by John Emory (B. Waugh and T. Mason, 1835); page 249.

QUESTIONS

1. Why is the prophet instructed to correct the people in such a way (Isaiah 58:1)? What is the complaint of the people? What is God's complaint?

2. What is the problem with the way the people are seeking God (Isaiah 58:2-3)?

3. How is our relationship with God affected by our relationship with others (Isaiah 58:3-4)?

4. What is self-affliction? What does it mean to "[bend] one's head like a reed" (Isaiah 58:5)? How does a modern believer apply this to the practices of prayer and fasting?

5. How do our prayers affect our priorities? How do our priorities affect our prayers?

6. Of what do the people need to be healed (Isaiah 58:8)? Of what do Christians today need to be healed? Of what do *you* need to be healed?

7. What are the promises of Isaiah 58:11-12? What are the conditions of these promises?

8. Do God's people trample the Sabbath today? Why does God take this sin so seriously (Isaiah 58:13)?

9. Why do spiritual disciplines such as fasting often seem like they're for the spiritually elite?

10. In the past, how have you experienced fasting during Lent? If you gave something up, why did you choose to give up what you did? What steps can you take to increase the practice of fasting? What are the challenges you anticipate?

4

THE PRACTICE OF FASTING
FINDING FREEDOM THROUGH DISCIPLINE

SCRIPTURE
LUKE 4:1-21

[1]Jesus returned from the Jordan River full of the Holy Spirit, and was led by the Spirit into the wilderness. [2]There he was tempted for forty days by the devil. He ate nothing during those days and afterward Jesus was starving. [3]The devil said to him, "Since you are God's Son, command this stone to become a loaf of bread."

[4]Jesus replied, "It's written, People won't live only by bread."[1]

[5]Next the devil led him to a high place and showed him in a single instant all the kingdoms of the world. [6]The devil said, "I will give you this whole domain and the glory of all these kingdoms. It's been entrusted to me and I can give it to anyone I want. [7]Therefore, if you will worship me, it will all be yours."

---

1 Deuteronomy 8:3

[8]Jesus answered, "It's written, You will worship the Lord your God and serve only him."[2]

[9]The devil brought him into Jerusalem and stood him at the highest point of the temple. He said to him, "Since you are God's Son, throw yourself down from here; [10]for it's written: He will command his angels concerning you, to protect you [11]and they will take you up in their hands so that you won't hit your foot on a stone."[3]

[12]Jesus answered, "It's been said, Don't test the Lord your God."[3] [13]After finishing every temptation, the devil departed from him until the next opportunity.

[14]Jesus returned in the power of the Spirit to Galilee, and news about him spread throughout the whole countryside. [15]He taught in their synagogues and was praised by everyone.

[16]Jesus went to Nazareth, where he had been raised. On the Sabbath he went to the synagogue as he normally did and stood up to read. [17]The synagogue assistant gave him the scroll from the prophet Isaiah. He unrolled the scroll and found the place where it was written:

[18]The Spirit of the Lord is upon me,
because the Lord has anointed me.

---

2 Deuteronomy 6:13
3 Deuteronomy 6:16

He has sent me to preach good news to the poor,

to proclaim release to the prisoners

and recovery of sight to the blind,

to liberate the oppressed,

[19]and to proclaim the year of the Lord's favor.4

[20]He rolled up the scroll, gave it back to the synagogue assistant, and sat down. Every eye in the synagogue was fixed on him. [21]He began to explain to them, "Today, this scripture has been fulfilled just as you heard it."

INSIGHT AND IDEAS

As I've mentioned, running has become a spiritual discipline for me. Forcing my body to do something that it doesn't want to do has shaped me spiritually as well as physically. When I started running this time around (you see, I've started and stopped running more times than I care to recount), I did so at the invitation of a friend who sent a message to all of the women she knew in our town who ran, wanted to run, or hung out with people who ran. She unwittingly started a running "club" that we dubbed "Sole Sisters." In fact, she was reluctant to call it a club, so she used quotation marks around it just to remind all of us that this thing was a grand experiment. I thanked her one time for starting the "club" and she laughed, saying, "I'm glad that

---

4 Isaiah 61:1-2; 58:6

you're enjoying it, but I originally did it because I needed accountability for myself. I wanted to run a half-marathon, but I knew I wouldn't do it if I had to do it all on my own."

When the running club started, I was looking for some accountability myself for exercise. I have struggled with my weight my entire life and was staring down numbers on the scale that were placing me far into the obese category. On a sweltering day in July, before the sun was up, looking around at a group of twenty- and thirty-something women (nearly all of whom were already fit), I trudged up and down the streets of our town, huffing and puffing, sweating and (nearly) swearing, and (re)learning to breathe. I'm sure that it was painful to watch; but thankfully, none of these sweet women pointed out that my clothes were not typical runner attire, my shoes were also used for yard work, and my time was barely better than speed-walking the route.

And yet I ran. Four days a week for two to four miles for those first 6 months, I ran. I bought some new shoes that supported me better, built friendships with the "Sole Sisters," and was mindful of the way that our physical health is at the core of our psychological and spiritual health.

As I rolled out of bed during those hot, and then very cold, mornings, I was reminded daily that discipline is hard. But even today, two half-marathons later, I can easily start to talk myself out of going for a run, sometimes even as little as two miles into the workout. But when I submit to the process, when I follow through with the action, even when

I don't want to follow through, only then do I find the strength for the task ahead.

FASTING AND TEMPTATION

Such it is with fasting. Fasting requires submission, discipline, and resolve. It means that we must individually stand up to temptation. Temptation to feel sorry for ourselves, to give up, to give in to weakness. Sometimes I imagine Jesus enduring temptation when I find myself tempted. I think about the ways that Jesus stood up to physical, relational, and psychological temptation.

The story of Jesus' being tempted in the desert is a familiar one. It is one that we learn as children and often fail to plumb the depths of as adults because it is so familiar. We often see Jesus standing strong in the face of temptation and think that he was tempted at his weakest moment; but I would offer that I think that during his time of prolonged fasting, he was at his strongest. You see, fasting creates clarity, defines priorities, and builds resolve. One of the fruits of the Spirit is self-control. Self-control is strengthened through the refining process of fasting. In this sense, it's not just about food. Food is generally the object of our fast, but it is not the focus. The focus is a life united with Christ.

Jesus entered the fast just after his baptism, when he was "full of the Holy Spirit" (verse 1). And it was the Holy Spirit who led him into the wilderness. I imagine Jesus, high from the affirmation of his identity. There was a voice from heaven who revealed that identity, if there ever was any question: "You are my Son, whom I dearly love; in you I find happiness" (Luke 3:22). This experience for Jesus was important, and I think that it's important for us. You see, before we do anything—any holy acts, any Christian service, and spiritual discipline—we must come face-to-face with the reality of our identity. We each have an individual identity of course, but we also have a corporate one. Our identity as humans means that we are weak, vulnerable, and often resistant to discipline. Our identity as Christians, however, tells us that we are God's children, beloved, and worthy of Christ's sacrifice. It is these two aspects of our identity that are held in tension when fasting.

The 40 days that Jesus spent fasting in the wilderness is reminiscent of another length of 40. When Moses lead the people out of slavery in Egypt, he lead them into a period of 40 years of wandering in the wilderness. It didn't take them 40 years to walk, so there was something important that happened during those 40 years. A new generation of Israelites was born, and the generation who had been unfaithful in that golden calf worship incident passed away (with the exception of a few noted faithful: Caleb, Joshua). What also happened was that the hearts of the people were cultivated to be faithful. Now, of course, the conquest and settlement of the Promised Land wasn't the kind of process that we want to emulate, but the imagery is clear: The number 40 in the wilderness evokes within our minds a release from slavery. This interchange between Jesus and his tempter just reveals to us a sense of what was at the heart of Jesus after his 40 days of fasting.

The first temptation preyed upon Jesus' physical weakness. In fact, the text says, "Jesus was starving" (Luke 4:2). The offer was even a good one: "Since you are God's Son, command this stone to become a loaf of bread" (Luke 4:3). Jesus' Sonship had been affirmed, so this was not outside of the possibility for him. He had the power to do it, and his fast was drawing to a close. The temptation, according to Henri Nouwen, in his priceless little book called *In the Name of Jesus: Reflections on Christian Leadership,* was to be relevant, to meet a need. Granted, it was a very legitimate need, but it was a shortcut and one that would exploit his creative power. Jesus put the temptation in its proper perspective by reminding the devil that *"People won't live only by bread,"* an allusion to the 40 years of wilderness wandering and relying on the manna from heaven that God provided (Deuteronomy 8:3).

The second temptation was one that Nouwen called the "temptation to be popular." The ways of the world were at the fingertips of the devil. He is the one who makes the world stand up and take notice. Jesus was offered dominion and glory over all the kingdoms of the world (Luke 4:6). Clearly, the path that Jesus would take would not be lined with popularly, dominion, or glory. Rather, he would take the way of the servant. His response reorients the tempter to the truth of who really reigns, *"You will worship the Lord your God and serve only him"* (Luke 4:8).

The third temptation revealed a smarter devil. He used the words of Scripture against Jesus: "Since you are God's Son, throw yourself down from here; for it's written, *He will* command his angels concerning you, to protect you and they will take you up in their hands so that you won't hit your foot on a stone" (Luke 4:9-10). It is a reference to Psalm 91, a passage about the trust that the psalmist had in God. However, Jesus underscores that the devil's ploys are not about trust but about doubt. "Don't test the Lord your God," Jesus says (Luke 4:12). Nouwen calls this the "temptation to be spectacular."

In each of these temptations, the devil points out a truth—Jesus' was indeed the Son of God and Satan does have the ability to rule the kingdoms of the world—but it wasn't the most important truth. Even as Jesus was tempted to be relevant, popular, and spectacular, he resisted through the strength of the Holy Spirit and the power of God's Word. And that power is made available to us as well. We are able to cultivate it through the practice of fasting.

PREPARING TO FAST

Are you ready now to step into a fast? As was mentioned, the Lenten fast is often one's first exposure to the particulars of fasting. The time period of Lent (40 days plus Sundays) should not be lost on us. While most of us endure the Lenten season without our chocolate, our pop, our TV, or maybe with a new spiritual practice, the challenge of abstaining from food is ever before us when we consider fasting.

I offer a few places to get started with the practice of fasting. I would also add a caution. Concerning fasting, the point is not to "complete the fast" but rather to connect with God. It isn't about restricting food; it's about opening up one's heart to God's still, steady voice that meets us in the desert. It isn't about ascetic practices that make us more holy because of others in history who have practiced them; it's about finding a freedom on the other side of discipline. In the midst of the weakness, we encounter the strength to endure the challenges that we face. Unfortunately, I've also seen people use fasting as a source of pride, and even (although very rarely) as a cleverly shrouded eating disorder. Enter a practice of fasting being sober-minded and spiritually open. That being said, here is some practical advice for you to get started.

THE TIME FACTOR

Determine a length of time that is appropriate for your fast. My most common fasting practice is what's known as the "Wesley Fast" and is from after dinner one night until mid-afternoon (or some say dinner) the following day. I practice this once a week. John Wesley often did it twice a week.

Consider whether you want to engage a partial fast (perhaps consisting of consuming only clear liquids—chicken broth or juice or merely eating vegetables or fruit and water) or a complete fast and abstaining from all food, except water. A fast that doesn't include drinking water is not advisable.

Substitute times of eating and preparing food with prayer. John Wesley, ever the champion of fasting, reminded us of the connection between the two.

Let us always join fervent prayer with fasting—pouring out our souls before God; confessing our sins; humbling ourselves; laying open all of our needs, all our guiltiness, and helplessness. This is a time for expanding our prayers— even our Lord fasted and prayed.

FASTING AND YOUR BODY

Pay attention to your body. Although your body has been conditioned to feel a "pang of hunger," what you feel in the beginning of a short-term fast is probably not physiological hunger. Our bodies have a natural reserve to carry us through times when we don't receive the nutrition we need, so set aside the urge to eat during the time that you've appointed. The pangs will go away, and you will find that you will actually have an increased focus and sense of purpose in what you are undertaking. Depending on the length of a fast, physical weakness will come. I usually limit physical activity during a fast that lasts more than a day.

When I've fasted, I've often felt irritable, impatient, and other emotions that make me a little less pleasant to be around others. I've learned that recognizing this is actually part of the spiritual power of fasting. All of those feelings aren't caused by fasting from food; they're under the surface and revealed by the spiritual practice. And God can shape and soften these feelings by the power of the Holy Spirit.

AN ONGOING SPIRITUAL PRACTICE

Fasting, for me, has become a spiritual practice to which I look forward. There have been times over the years that I've gotten out of the habit of fasting because of scheduled activities that "required" me to join a group and eat. I've learned that usually, even in such activities, more often than not, I can excuse myself and connect with God. You see, when I do not practice it, I feel the impact in my soul. Much like running, it is something in which I have been able to build stamina. The stamina is somewhat physical, but it is mostly spiritual. I'm able to engage more deeply with God through prayer, journaling, and reading Scripture when I'm fasting regularly. My physical body has learned to let go of the addiction of food at the hours that I had conditioned my body to crave food, and it has learned to be satisfied with spiritual food. As Jesus said, *"People won't live only by bread."* Life isn't found in calories, in vitamins, in nutrients; athough those things sustain life. Rather, life is found in submitting our lives to God, in taking on the life of Christ, and in putting one foot after another, day after day.

While each of us are individual Christians running our own race, our communities around us encourage us, cast important visions for us, and give us accountability. There's nothing quick about a fast; but for someone who endures it, the life of a faithful Christian, one who can stand up to the temptations that come our way, awaits a victory worth far more than the successes of this world.

QUESTIONS

1. Why was it important for the Spirit to lead Jesus into the wilderness (Luke 4:1)? What does it mean to be led by the Spirit?

2. What purpose might fasting have served as Jesus was being tempted by the devil for 40 days?

3. What is the difference between testing and temptation?

4. How does Jesus respond to each of the devil's temptations? Why, do you think, does Jesus answer in this way? How can Christians apply this today when we face temptation?

5. Evaluate the devil's claim in Luke 4:6-7? Would this be a serious temptation for Jesus? Why, or why not?

6. The devil departs Jesus "until the next opportunity" (verse 13). What are some conclusions we might draw from this verse about the nature of temptation?

7. How is Jesus' mission in Luke 4:18-9 our mission?

8. Why does fasting help build resolve?

9. In what ways might fasting seem counterintuitive?

10. What can the church do to increase awareness about the importance of fasting in a believer's life? What can individuals do? What, do you think, would happen if an overwhelming majority of Christians were to fast on a regular basis?

CONVERGE

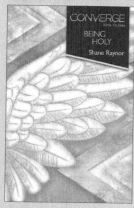

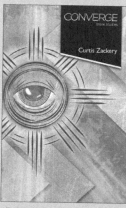

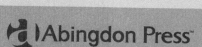

CPSIA information can be obtained at www.ICGtesting.com
Printed in the USA
LVOW01s1940110714

393963LV00002B/2/P